MYSTE

NUTSHELL

The World's Most Concise Guide to
Mystery and Suspense Writing

by

JOHN McALEER

and

ANDREW McALEER

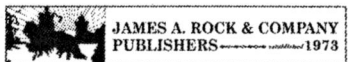

JAMES A. ROCK & COMPANY
PUBLISHERS ━━━━━ established 1973

Mystery Writing in a Nutshell:
The World's Most Concise Guide to Mystery and Suspense Writing
by John McAleer and Andrew McAleer

JAMES A. ROCK & COMPANY, PUBLISHERS

Mystery Writing in a Nutshell:
The World's Most Concise Guide to Mystery and Suspense Writing
copyright ©2007 by Andrew McAleer

Special contents of this edition copyright ©2007
by James A. Rock & Co., Publishers

Address comments and inquiries to:

James A. Rock & Company, Publishers
9710 Traville Gateway Drive, #305
Rockville, MD 20850

E-mail:
jrock@rockpublishing.com   lrock@rockpublishing.com
Internet URL: www.rockpublishing.com

Trade Paperback ISBN: 1-59663-505-3

Library of Congress Control Number: 2005937821

Printed in the United States of America

First Edition: 2007

Visit Andrew McAleer at

www.Crimestalkers.com

Other books by John McAleer

Rex Stout: A Majesty's Life
from James A. Rock & Co., Publishers
(original title *Rex Stout: A Biography*)

Ralph Waldo Emerson: Days of Encounter

Coign of Vantage

Unit Pride

Other books by Andrew McAleer

Double Endorsement

Bait and Switch

Appearance of Counsel

MYSTERY WRITING
IN A NUTSHELL

To
Alice M. Delaney
and
James A. Woods, S.J.
Always on the case.

ACKNOWLEDGMENTS

None of my father's books, this one included, could have been written without my mother, Ruth Delaney McAleer's devotion to husband and family. I thank her and, on behalf of my father, I thank her. A debt of gratitude is also due our publishers, James and Lynne Rock, whose commitment to the crime fiction genre is a matter of sound record. I wish also to thank Paula Munier, Kris Neri, Edward D. Hoch, Robert B. Parker, Margaret McLean, Uwe Stender, and Robin Moore for their faith in this project and hence, the many projects you, the reader, are about to blueprint.

Table of Contents

CHAPTER 4

*My theory is that people who don't like
mystery stories are anarchists.*

—Rex Stout

FOREWORD

The earliest book on mystery writing, *The Technique of the Mystery Story* by Carolyn Wells, was published nearly a century ago in 1913. Wells had written only four mystery novels at that time, though she went on to publish nearly eighty more during the course of a long and successful career. This pioneering volume, a product of The Home Correspondence School, was 336 pages long, and a later revision added another hundred pages.

There have been scores of how-to books published since then, many by well-known mystery writers. But to my mind they all suffer from being too long. Today's beginning mystery writer wants to *begin*, and she or he doesn't need to plow through hundreds of pages to learn the necessary fundamentals. It seems to me that the book you hold in your hand, *Mystery Writing in a Nutshell*, has the distinct advantage of being both authoritative and concise.

Its authors, John McAleer and his son Andrew McAleer, have devoted their distinguished careers to the teaching and writing of crime fiction. John McAleer, winner of the Edgar Allan Poe Award for his definitive biography of Rex Stout, taught crime fiction to some of our leading authors during nearly four decades at Boston College. Andrew McAleer has followed in his father's footsteps as Professor of Crime Fiction at the same college. In addition to teaching, both father and son have published mysteries of their own.

In these pages you'll find a concise synopsis of the knowledge the McAleers have garnered and passed along to their students. There are valuable hints on getting ideas, plotting, researching your setting, hooking the reader, choosing a snappy title, and hiding clues in plain sight. The authors emphasize the importance of reading everything, something I always tell would-be writers.

After all these years, I still learned a few things myself from these pages. I'm sure you will too.

—Edward D. Hoch
New York

INTRODUCTION

In the 1960s, my father, John McAleer, introduced a crime fiction course to the Boston College curriculum. According to my father's research, it was one of the first, if not the only, college-credit course of its kind in America. As for myself, my own education in the mystery genre began long before college.

Our home was filled wall-to-wall with the Golden Age of Mystery and beyond: R. Austen Freeman, Agatha Christie, Sir Arthur Conan Doyle, Freeman Wills Crofts, Dorothy Sayers, Dashiell Hammett, and Rex Stout, among many others, lurked in every dark corner of our homestead. Always on the lookout for new talent to enjoy and share with his students, my father, in later years, took to Robert B. Parker, Dennis Lehane, Gregory Mcdonald, Rhys Bowen, W.J. Burley, and William Tapply. And as his "Watson," I did my best to keep pace. The mystery genre became the "baseball" my father and I shared.

Entering Boston College as a freshman in the fall of 1986, I enrolled in my father's Detective Fiction and Espionage course. Seventeen years later, I found myself coteaching The Master Sleuths with him. I don't think it was until then that I realized how much my father had tricked me into learning. As a result, I became the quintessential novice teacher. I assumed that my "eager" students would be familiar with the crime fiction authors, crime fiction's various sub-genres, and the crime fiction nomenclature that was by now elementary to me. I was mistaken.

It was a shock to learn that many of the students had no knowledge of red herrings or police procedurals, and had no idea what a hard-boiled dick was. By now I had published my second mystery. I started to jot down the technical rules my father had taught me about what should be or is expected to be in a mystery novel, because I thought I might get a lecture out of the deal. I expected to cobble out a dozen rules or so, but the rules, like the list of suspects in a Christie novel, kept growing. "Don't forget to add 'this' or 'that' to your lecture," my father would remind me.

As the course progressed, I began to write down more and more of my father's rules and I have been honing them ever since, organizing and simplifying them for my students and emerging authors of the mystery genre. The result was a lifetime of rules my father had passed on to me. Rules gathered from reading, studying, teaching, and interviewing, corresponding with, and working with—cheek by jowl—some of the world's most successful authors in the field, like Rex Stout, James M. Cain, Lady Mary Stewart, Gregory Mcdonald, June Thomson, Robert B. Parker, Jane Langton, Rick Boyer, Dennis Lehane, William Tapply, Jeremiah Healy, and Katherine Hall Page. It is my hope—and my father's as well, I know—that after a careful study of *Mystery Writing in a Nutshell*, you will not only be a mystery scholar and devotee of the genre, but a successful mystery author as well. Good hunting, Holmes!

—Andrew McAleer
Boston College, 2007

CHAPTER ONE

Creating
Suspense and Action

1.1 What is a Mystery?

One of crime fiction's most successful publishers, editors, and authors, Otto Penzler, defines *mystery* as, "Any short work of fiction in which a crime or the threat of a crime is central to the theme or the plot. It is a broad definition, covering detective, espionage, suspense, and crime fiction. Horror or supernatural is *not* included."

1.2 What is Suspense?

Suspense is achieved by maintaining sustained anxiety created by a state of mental uncertainty coupled with a constant desire for decision or resolution. Or, more simply put by Stephanie Kay Bendel (*Making Crime Pay*), suspense is "anxiety created by uncertainty." According to suspense novelist Charlotte Armstrong (*Catch-as-Catch-Can*), suspense is made up of *fear, time,* and *hope.*

You must keep your readers anxious throughout the whole story. They must want to know how the conflict or conflicts will be resolved. Additionally, make your readers anxious about how your sleuth intends—*against all odds*—to bring about the resolution.

1.3 Time Elements

Put your protagonist in a fight against *time* preferably while on the horns of a dilemma. Make it believable.

For example, why must the crime or mystery be solved in 48 hours?

> *Create a time element:*
>> "Mr. President, the terrorists have given you 48 hours to make your decision."
>
> *Create a dilemma:*
>> "If you answer 'no,' then they will begin detonating dirty bombs in every major U.S. city. If you answer 'yes,' then America will have to surrender."

Now, how will your protagonist, as logicians sometimes say, "escape between the horns of a dilemma"?

Create a "ticking time bomb" under the seat or a kidnapper who gives you 24 hours to come up with the ransom money—or else. Make your story as much about racing against time as it is about catching the bad guy!

Think Quicksand
> Your protagonist has only so much time to escape and is constantly thwarted by limited resources

and/or seemingly endless roadblocks that frustrate her race against time. Moreover, for whatever reason, your sleuth is the *only* person who can resolve the conflict. If *she* doesn't do it or can't do it, the kidnapper will kill the little boy, the serial killer will kill again and again and again, the ticking time bomb will blow up innocent children, an innocent young man with his whole life ahead of him will go to the gas chamber, a slick, murderous politician will be reelected and continue his nefarious ways.

1.4 The Murder Connection

Two seemingly *unconnected* murders can build tension and create suspense in your story. For example, a gangster is murdered in Chicago and a maple syrup farmer is murdered in Vermont. Why? How are these two murders connected? These are questions that your sleuth will have to answer in order to solve the puzzle and put the bad guy behind bars.

1.5 Action

It's true that items like car chases, fist fights, and machine guns will enhance the action in your story, but action is not *limited* to violence. There are other types of *action*—activities that bring your characters and scenes to life like: brushing teeth, feeding chickens, opening and pouring wine, sharpening a pencil, getting a haircut, making lemonade, watching a flock of birds, loading a .38, tending to roses, changing a baby, etc.

For example:
> Create action during a conversation: While your sleuth is questioning a suspect, make the suspect wash a car or change a flat tire.

Ask yourself, "What could this character be doing other than sitting at a desk with her hands laced?" If the scene calls for her to sit at a desk, then what might she be *doing* to create a sense of action for the reader?

1.6 Pacing

Avoid prolonged descriptions, especially those not germane to solving the mystery. As a rule, every part of your story should ultimately serve the purpose of solving the crime.

For example:
> Instead of placing a scene around a conventional dinner table, have your characters discuss details while running on a treadmill, chopping wood, taking out the garbage, or sharpening a knife.

Something should always be happening. Create *movement, movement, movement!* Avoid scenes that contribute little to the story.

We live in a sound-bite society, so make scenes quick, powerful, and productive. Short, snappy dialogue can be the linchpin of good *pacing*.
> "Go ahead, make my day."
> "Hasta la vista, baby."
> "Here's looking at you, kid."

Tip: Make your chapters short. Your work will predominately appeal to the lunchtime and public transportation reader. Multi-Edgar Allan Poe Award winner Gregory Mcdonald has a one-page first chapter in *Fletch, Too*. Robert B. Parker, Georges Simenon, and James M. Cain are also brilliant at writing short, effective chapters.

1.7 Title

The title of your work is crucial. If your book title is too "cryptic," too long or just plain boring, then your book may not attract a publisher, an editor, a bookshop owner, or the fussy browser. Like the "narrative hook" (next chapter), the title may not come to you until well after the book is finished.

New York Times best-selling author Robin Moore said that *The French Connection* was originally called *The Patsy Fuca Case* and that Little, Brown had actually printed up some *Patsy Fuca* dust jackets. Moore hated this and kept telling himself that there needed to be some "French connection" in the title. Then, while walking down Newbury Street in Boston, it hit him — *The French Connection!* He ran back up Newbury, through the Public Garden and Boston Common, up Beacon Hill and over to the offices of Little, Brown, where, reluctantly, his editor agreed to call the book *The French Connection.*

In 1935, Rex Stout submitted "The League of the White Feather" for publication. The title went through a long process of evolution (including magazine serialization) but was finally published with the excellent title of *The League of Frightened Men*.

Tip: If your title is too long, people may not remember it. Short and snappy titles often make for good marketing. Sometimes a "cryptic" title will work, however, if the title itself is a bit mysterious but *suggestive*. Prospective readers might become curious and want to know more. In that case, your title *itself* will create suspense (1.2).

1.8   Have a Smoke, Doll Face
Smoking is often overdone and a poor excuse for action. If you have a character who smokes, make sure it fits the character's personality. Does your story take place in Hollywood during the Truman Administration? Then perhaps it makes sense to have people smoke throughout the story.

1.9   Hitchcock and the McGuffin
Edgar Award-winner William L. DeAndrea states in his *Encyclopedia Mysteriosa* that a good "McGuffin" is essential. The term "McGuffin" was introduced (or at least popularized) by movie director Alfred Hitchcock. According to Hitchcock, the "McGuffin" is the thing in the story that the characters "care" about. In *The Maltese Falcon* it's the "black bird," in *The Big Sleep* it's Rusty Regan, and in *The Hound of the Baskervilles* it's the curse. As DeAndrea points out, the McGuffin is

the "prize to win or the doom to be avoided that sets the actual plot in motion."

1.10 On- and Off-Stage Murders

Will your readers just *hear* about the victim/murder or are they going to *witness* the murder and/or surrounding events? If your readers only *hear* about the event, then this is called an "off-stage murder." If your readers actually *see* the murder or find themselves on the scene when the murder takes place, then this is deemed an "on-stage murder." For example, in *Coign of Vantage*, three members of a Boston literary society die horribly before the book begins. The sleuth, Austin Layman, and the reader are simply told about the deaths. These murders are off-stage murders. In the Prologue of *Coign*, however, the reader witnesses a horrible murder. This is an on-stage murder.

Both on-stage and off-stage murders have their advantages. Off-stage can enhance mystery and suspense. Like our sleuth, readers want to know *why* and/or *how* the victim was murdered (or, sometimes, if a murder actually took place). Hence, the reader is presented immediately with a puzzle.

On-stage murders provide readers an opportunity to witness events through the eyes of the sleuth, narrator, or, sometimes, the actual murderer. On-stage murders sometimes provide "procedural" information by showing police and detectives processing the murder scene. On-stage murders create a natural anxiety by forming a "bond" between the reader and the victim.

The reader shares the pain, fear, and struggles of the victim and the hunt for the culprit often becomes more personal. It is sometimes effective to have both off-stage and on-stage murders in your novel.

CHAPTER TWO

The Story
& The Hook

2.1 What is a Story?

Famous Hollywood producer George Abbott
(*Damned Yankees*) dissected the story into three acts:

> *FIRST ACT*: Put your protagonist in a tree.
> *SECOND ACT:* Throw rocks at your
>   protagonist.
> *THIRD ACT:* Help your protagonist down
>   from the tree.

2.2 Back Story

A back story is a story that begins before the main
story. Your story should have one.

In Sue Grafton's *"A" is for Alibi,* readers learn in the
first sentence of the novel that protagonist, Kinsey
Millhone, a California-based private investigator, is

twice divorced *before* the story began. Additionally, we learn in the second sentence that Millhone killed someone two days *before* the story began. Readers know immediately that characterization and plot will pivot on these "back stories." At the outset, we want to know more about Millhone and this mysterious killing.

In Elmore Leonard's *Freaky Deaky* we learn in the opening of the novel that, for some reason, protagonist Chris Mankowski is leaving the Bomb Squad. The circumstances behind his departure took place *before* the story began and if we want to know what they are we will have to read on.

In Michael Connelly's *The Lincoln Lawyer,* a big money ne'er-do-well gets hooked for aggravated assault and attempted rape *before* the story begins. Now it's up to veteran defense attorney Mickey Haller to pull off a "not guilty" verdict and unravel the strange nexus between this present case and a murder case he lost some years ago.

When reading novels try to pick out the back story and note how it is introduced.

2.3 Narrative Hook
How does your *first chapter/act/story* begin? Why would a reader read on? Will your opening sentence grab the reader's attention?

There was a time when a publisher or agent might have given you a few pages to get your story going. Later, that offer became a page and, later still, only a paragraph. Today, you are on your own.

Your first sentence must *hook the reader* because books are now competing with the internet, cable TV, TiVo, DirecTV, large mortgages, soccer practice, etc. However, if you can't find that "perfect" opening sentence when you begin your novel, don't let this deter you. Your *narrative hook* may not come until you have completed the book. It can come at any time during the process of writing and editing your story. The important thing is to get the story written.

In my book, *Double Endorsement*, the first chapter was the last thing I wrote. Likewise, in my father's mystery, *Coign of Vantage*, the prologue was the last section he wrote. A few years ago I had the opportunity to hear multi-Shamus Award winner Jeremiah Healy address the Boston Authors Club. He stated that honing the first three to four pages of your book is essential.

Read your first pages out loud and hear how they sound.

Tip: Browse the crime fiction section of a bookstore or library and read the first sentence of some mystery novels. See if the author *hooks* you. If so, then what techniques or words worked? By the same token, if the author *doesn't hook* you, try to determine exactly why.

Tip: Examine synopses provided for rental movies. These synopses are written by experts whose *job* is to hook viewers into renting the movie.

CHAPTER THREE

Fodder for Writing
(Ideas for Getting Ideas)

3.1 Law Enforcement

Talk to local law enforcement officials about their daily grind or their booking and arresting procedures. They can offer a wealth of information. Just have questions ready for them.

And when you do visit the station, note the *physical* layout. What is the size of a cell? The waiting area? Are the off-duty cops playing Crazy Eights or complaining about how bad the coffee is? Is this an Andy Griffith-type jail or the Middlesex County holding cell in Massachusetts, where there are no windows or openings except a small crack for sliding in a boxed lunch and a milk carton.

Don't wait for jury duty. Spend a whole day in a local court and note the pressure there is to "move the docket along." Listen to the dialogue and note the dynamics among the judge, the prosecutors, the defense attorneys, the victim witness advocates, the defendants, the probation officers, and the clerks.

And this doesn't hold true just for law enforcement. If you want to create a scene that takes place in a horse's stable, then visit a horse's stable. Need a saw mill? Then visit one. An ice house? Then visit an ice house.

3.2 Occupational Jargon/Argot

Each job has its own terms and language. Try to learn some of that language. This will help you create authentic-sounding characters.

Sometimes the language is so job-specific that the reader may not know what you are talking about. A good way around this is to have your sleuth not know what it means either. She'll have to ask the coroner what he means by CHF—chronic heart failure. Or perhaps your sleuth knows but the "Watson" counterpart does not. Here your sleuth can explain its meaning to the "Watson" and therefore, the reader.

Some terms of the art are self-explanatory but colorful. For example, a nurse characterizing a patient as a "train wreck," a custodian in a nursing home saying that he's on "puddle patrol," or a bent-nose type saying he has to make a pair of "cement shoes."

3.3 Know Your Venue

Get to know the community you are writing about.

- Local color, odd villager
- Local haunts
- Local newspaper
- Local politics
- Local customs and sayings
- Local names: visit local monuments or cemeteries
- Local history
- Local legends or folklore
- Local weather
- Local shops
- Local foods
- Local wildlife, etc.
- Local businesses
- Local "families"

3.4 Stay Young

Talk to kids and learn the latest trends and slang. When I read my father's *Coign of Vantage* now, I laugh at a scene where a college student is wearing a pair of Reebok sneakers. The book came out when I was in college and Reeboks were my chosen footwear at the time. Little did I know that I was literary fodder for my father—or at least my *feet* were.

3.5 Catalogues and Web Sites

A good way to keep track of clothing styles is to consult mail-order catalogues and commercial web sites. And, if you're like my father, who is colorblind, you may not know exactly how to coordinate outfits. A quick gander at a catalogue or web site can help you dress your characters.

Be sure to attire your characters appropriately. Consider Brooks Brothers, Just My Size, Victoria's Secret, Target, K-Mart, etc.

A look out the window or a trip to the mall may also help. Are you picking the kids up from school today? While waiting for them, note what other kids are wearing these days.

Tip: Always be in "writer-overdrive." Everything you do, see, hear, taste, or touch is possible fodder for writing. A trip to the market is no longer just about getting that two-for-one deal, but also becomes a field-op for absorbing the latest trends in food and technology.

3.6 News in Brief

Many times the best stories are not found in the front page headlines. Check out those small notices in the "News in Brief" or "Our Town" section of the newspaper, where small-town "incidents" and politics are reported. This can be a great source of ideas. For example, "Is someone really 'out to get' the Tree Warden, the president of the Cabot Cove's Newcomers' Tea, or the treasurer of the Historic Greenville Community Group?"

3.7 Brochures

Did you once visit a cave in Bermuda but have now forgotten all the details? Perhaps you'd love to incorporate a scene in your mystery there, but you just don't trust your memory. Well, you should have grabbed a *brochure* while you were there. These little freebies will usually cover the location, legend, discovery date, and other (usually timeless) details about "items and scenes of interest" when you travel.

Brochures also have specific language and tone that you can incorporate into your writing.

The internet is a also great source, especially for secondary facts, But there is something special about a brochure that can bring your scene to life and help you visualize your characters "on location."

3.8 Maps

Maps are another good writer's resource. You may want to name roads, streets, and intersections and then follow your detective as he travels through Boston or LA side streets.

Obtain a map of the city and lay out your detective's route. "Drive" with her and share the specifics with your reader. Then drive her route yourself, noting local landmarks and determining how long the drive takes. Are there any traffic hot spots, unwanted stop signs, or potholes? If your protagonist experiences the same sweaty or icy traffic dilemmas as the locals do, readers will elevate her to the highest pedestal. The reader is in the thick of it just like your sleuth, and your sleuth is in the thick of it just like your reader.

For example:
"Polly turned south on Taylor Road. Just beyond Allen's Tire Shop, she hung a left and continued east past the now abandoned and decrepit Franklin Pierce Elementary School, dodging delivery trucks rumbling through the recently-industrialized district."
Take the reader along for the ride.

3.9 Weather Reports
Check the paper or *The Farmer's Almanac* for weather reports. Note how meteorologists describe the weather. You can adopt many of the words used in these reports and sound like a real pro.

As an exercise, take today's weather report from the newspaper and see if you can turn it into dialogue. Maybe you've got some blowhard meteorologist at a PTA meeting and he's bending someone's ear about low-pressure fronts coming in. Try the same exercise with the ingredients in a household cleaner. Now you can have a chemist or scientist or environmentalist bending someone's ear about the effects of "yellow number 5."

3.10 Read, Read, Read
Cereal boxes, directions, ingredients—ideas can come from anywhere at anytime. Read everything you can, not just mystery books.

Tip: Reading is the best way to learn how to write. My father was taught at Harvard that you can ordinarily learn more about writing in one hour of reading than you can in six hours of writing.

3.11 The Work Place

Look for ideas and characters that can be incorporated from your own personal job experiences. Think back to part-time jobs you held in high school or college. Let your characters benefit from what you know first-hand working as a retail clerk, custodian, lab tech, bartender, hairdresser, or executive administrative assistant.

3.12 Pets

It may be a good idea for your sleuth to have a pet such as a dog or cat. Right away, your sleuth will appeal to all dog lovers. Just make sure the pet does not slow down the action. Your sleuth should not spend five pages trying to get a dog sitter.

On the other hand, if you have an inordinate fear of dogs (or spiders, etc.), consider applying this phobia to one of your characters.

3.13 Food

Food, for whatever reason, is an important literary device in mysteries. Many people like to read about food. They also want to know about the restaurants your sleuth patronizes. If he's a good cook then they may want to know his recipes. If you know of a great restaurant, describe the dining experience so that aroma of the main fare is wafting off the pages.

Gather information when you go to a restaurant. Note the menu items and "specialities." Some places might give you a menu. Be sure to check the internet—many restaurants post their menus online these days. Does your sleuth fancy a unique sandwich? Remember, people still talk about Elvis' peanut butter and banana sandwiches.

William Tapply's lawyer-sleuth, Brady Coyne, loves restaurants and Tapply does an expert job of describing these eateries. Agatha Award winner Katherine Hall Page's stories, featuring protagonist Faith Fairchild, are chock full of gastronomical recipes as are the Nero Wolfe stories. In fact, both series have excellent cookbooks in their honor.

3.14 Music
Name the popular songs (composers, performers) which serve as a "backdrop" on the radio or in the nightclub where your sleuth is questioning a suspect. Elmore Leonard and Dennis Lehane do this quite well. And hey, when they make the movie based on your book, won't the songs you chose make a great soundtrack?

If you have a special interest in music (classical, jazz, etc.) then consider incorporating your knowledge and expertise in one of your characters.

3.15 Quotes
Swipe a few good quotes from Shakespeare, Alexander Pope, Dr. Samuel Johnson, Daniel Webster, U2, Bruce Springsteen, Robin Williams, etc. Just make sure you give credit where credit is due. If you use any words from a song or poem whose copyright has not

expired, you will have to get permission from the copyright owner. You may reference the title of a song or poem without permission.

Using scholarly quotes also makes reading your mystery an education for readers. Readers will feel good about this—aside from reading a fun, suspenseful book, they may have learned something.

Sir John Mortimer's character, Rumple of the Bailey, often quotes classical poetry; Miss Marple, the Bible; and my father's character, Austin Layman, quotes Emerson.

3.16 Law
Knowledge of the law can be a good touch. Knowing the actual recitation of the *Miranda* warnings will impress readers and knowledge of jurisdictional differences is also important. Learn the distinction between burglary and robbery. (Houses get burglarized; people get robbed.) Your local library should have a copy of *Black's Law Dictionary*.

Warning:: If you are not writing a legal thriller then don't get bogged down in too much legalese. A turf war between the DA or Police Chief and your sleuth might be enough to display your awareness of criminal procedure. This dynamic can sometimes pit your sleuth not only against the bad guys but also against the fuzz. When your hero's getting squeezed from the bad guy and the law at the same time, this can add greatly to tension and character development.

3.17 Flowers

A basic knowledge of flowers and landscaping can help visualize a story. Note what time of year certain flowers or vegetables start to bud, break earth, come to fruition or begin to wither. What flowers are unique or indigenous to your setting?

3.18 Architecture

A basic knowledge of architecture can make your story three dimensional. Don't bog the reader down with too much detail. It is far more interesting, however, if a character lives in a brownstone, a ranch house, a box-framed farmhouse, or an old Cape rather than just a "house."

Interior details add dimension and interest as well. Can your sleuth hear the old lady clacking her heels on the satin-finished hardwood floors as she readies the silver tea service? Or, does she just glide over the Oriental rugs and spook your sleuth?

3.19 Advertisements

Advertisements may contain colorful language that you can adopt. How does that beer, cigarette, or sirloin taste?

Is your shampoo "aristocratically manufactured"? Is your tape or CD collection "digitally re-mastered"?

Tip: As an exercise, try writing some advertising language into a dialogue with several characters.

3.20 Name that Food

Know a few key wines, cheeses, and main dishes. If someone grabs a hot dog make it a Fenway Frank or a Nathan's. A guy might have a Sterling or a Sam Adams Octoberfest. Create a character with epicurean standards who may demand 4C mint jelly with his Irish mutton. Little touches—like knowing which wines go with which foods, can give your story credibility. Think of the fussy character who insists on a particular wine to accompany his bluefish, or the two-fisted guy who finds himself at a formal event where he turns down champagne for a Bud.

CHAPTER FOUR

Voice, Voice, Voice

4.1 Setting

What is your setting? Think long and hard about this because it will dictate the tone and voice of your novel as well as the reader's expectation that you will provide realistic details.

Confinement of Investigation: Think of Christie's detective, Hercule Poirot, on a small island where there can be only so many suspects. Consider a cruise ship, a rural estate, a plane, a moving train, a country club, but only select settings you are familiar with or can recreate authentically.

Travel: Travel adds interest and motion to the story. Ask yourself, "Why might my Boston-based P.I. have to travel to Chicago?" Take your reader on a quick pop to Nova Scotia, Baltimore, or Holly-wood. Let your hero wander from town to town, commenting on the similarities and differences from the main setting. "I've always hated the DC suburbs for gumshoe work. It's impossible to find a cab and, should you luck-out, they'll never take you back to the city."

Exotic Locations. Consider the James Bond adventures. We expect Bond to take us places we may never visit—indeed may have never heard of. Again, here is an opportunity to "educate" and entertain readers while telling your story. Do not consider an exotic location, however, unless you feel confident to reproduce the specifics and atmosphere (mandatory) required for your setting.

4.2   Dialogue/Point of View (POV)

Pitch-perfect dialogue is both difficult and essential. Hone your skill in writing dialogue by reading the masters. Practice by converting a narrative paragraph to dialogue. Then reverse the process. Don't confuse readers by using ambiguous pronouns (Huh? Who said that?) and long, rambling exchanges, especially between more than two characters.

Remember that writing good dialogue is *not* necessarily how people converse in real life. And don't lose sight of the fact that the purpose of dialogue is to communicate information about your story and characters. Study experienced writers and analyze why their dialogue flows so realistically. Hemingway was praised for the dialogue in his novels. But when it was converted to the screen, directors found his writing awkward and it had to be re-written to make it sound "natural."

Go for quick, humorous, snappy parting shots! Your dialogue should touch the human heart. Dialogue is a great way to introduce description, clues, irony, subtext, slang, and your sleuth's defenses, prejudices, emotions, and philosophies. Dialogue can identify your character more than anything else. Know your character's "voice." Dialogue is something that writers hone for their entire careers.

Cherish the one-liners. Steal them from your children. Remember Shakespeare said that "brevity is the soul of wit." Or, in *Strunk and White*, "Brevity is a by-product of vigor."

Remember when that check-out girl made a nasty remark and three days later you came up with a great retort? Now, you have immediate revenge through your creative writing. The check-out girl now gives your sleuth the same nasty remark and he fires right back with the snappy retort you've invented. Writers are the sum total of their experiences. Now, no matter what happens—the good and the bad in life—it can become fodder for your writing. Make today's turmoil tomorrow's humor.

Tip: Do what Elmore Leonard did and read George V. Higgin's *The Friends of Eddie Coyle*. At one point during my correspondence, Leonard wrote to me, saying, "I was able to write an introduction to *The Friends of Eddie Coyle* because that book set me free. It loosened up my writing, taught me to get into scenes quicker and to concentrate more on a realistic sound in writing dialogue, what Higgins called 'the nuances of ordinary speech.' And to back Leonard up, *Life Magazine* said that Higgins could ". . .write dialogue so authentic it spits. . . ."

4.3   First-Person Narrative POV (Point of View)

Think of first-person POV as writing a journal. Have your sleuth actually talk as though this reader is his special friend and your sleuth is sharing something unique, maybe even confidential, to this and only this reader.

The first-person narrative is useful in answering the question, "Why does this story need to be told?" Think of James M. Cain's *The Postman Always Rings Twice* in which the convicted murderer confesses his story on death row to a priest. In *Double Indemnity*, the wounded murderer relates his story by recording the details into a Dictaphone—his final confession before dying.

4.4   Third-Person Narrative POV (Point of View)

The third-person point of view is the omniscient (all knowing) delivery. This type of narrative can give the author more freedom to actually enter the minds of all the characters because the narrator can be anywhere at any time.

The first-person narrative can be more restrictive because the story is told through the eyes of one character only—usually your sleuth. James M. Cain, however, felt that there was something more *real* about the first-person and that the third-person narrative requires a greater "suspension of disbelief."

When I asked William Tapply about POV, this is what he had to say:

McAleer: Not too long ago Poisoned Pen Press republished a fine edition of your first Brady Coyne novel, *Death at Charity Point* and in your updated Introduction you mention that the first-person narrative is what ultimately introduced you to Brady's voice. James M. Cain took the position that the first-person narrative has a ring of truth to it that the third-person does not. Would you agree with Cain's assessment?

Tapply: I think an author's choice of point-of-view is one of the most important writing decisions he can make — and, in my experience, it's rarely given serious thought by beginning writers. POV gives readers a place to stand and eyes and ears for experiencing the events of the story. First-person gives readers a specific person as a guide. Third-person gives them . . . an author. In fact, I stumbled on first-person by trial and error. When I tried it, it sounded right and felt comfortable. This makes sense. The first-person POV gives me a voice, a way of seeing the story's world. And it enables me to present a mystery honestly. With third-person, no matter how well done it is, readers are always aware of The Author out there manipulating things, pulling strings, revealing only what he wants to reveal, dipping into and out of the heads of various characters, sharing and withholding information at will. I think that's what Cain means by third-person lacking the complete honesty that a candid first-person narrator conveys. First-person is a conversation between a trustworthy narrator and trusting reader. It's really a speaking voice, not a written, literary voice.

And here is what James M. Cain shared with my father:

James M. Cain: . . . In the third-person, I don't care how good you are, or even if you're Sinclair Lewis, there come times when it seems as though you're making it up as you go along. To that extent, first-person narration *must* be respected. It has its limitations, and yet it always steps up things. I spend more time figuring why the character should be telling this fantastic thing, I have to figure that one out: What's he telling this for? In *The Postman Always Rings Twice*, it seemed simple enough, he had to *die*, and he wanted to leave some record of this love story between him and Cora, this girl who had helped him knock off her husband, and it all seemed so wonderful and beautiful. It seemed perfectly in character and plausible that he would be telling this story in a death house. For example, in *The Moth*, there didn't seem to be any good reason that this fellow would be telling the story, but he *did* tell it. I invented some reason that he'd be telling it ...

4.5 Tone

What is the *tone* of your mystery? Happy, sad, sunny, gray? Note the detail and incorporate seasonal changes. Venues with seasons often make a good settings for mysteries. The story may open near the end of summer. Then the action begins to gain momentum as the story moves into fall. When the foliage begins to wither and the temperature drops, the hurricane season begins and the reader senses impending doom with the arrival of the storm.

Or does the desert heat have everyone on edge? Is your sleuth a stranger to this kind of heat? Or consider cold, frigid, unyielding, monochromatic landscapes covered with snow and ice. Is this a hindrance or an aid to your protagonist? Your killer or bad guy?

4.6 Sight, Sound, Flavor, and Inflection

Sight. Enhance your story with visual details. Include flowers, colors, clothes, hair, flocks of birds, sunsets, breaking waves, and phases of the moon.

Sound. Don't stop with music or songs. Add chop saws, jackhammers, squealing tires, steeple clocks, skate boards, trains, chimes, wildlife, spitting, chug-ging domestic beer, sizzling bacon, or screaming children. I heard Beatle producer George Martin speak at Harvard, and he said that when John Lennon wrote the song *Being for the Benefit of Mr. Kite*—about a fair ground—Lennon told him that he wanted to "Hear the sawdust on the floor."

Flavor. The smell and taste of food: savory, bitter, cloying, salty, earthy. Consider coffee, beer, fizzy sodas, egg creams, wine, liquors along with local, foreign and exotic flavors.

Inflection. Listen to how folks speak in a particular area. Think of the rapid Boston accent or the slow Southern twang. What are local sayings? What are kids saying these days and who are they saying it to? Not to mom and dad.

4.7 Similes & Metaphors

Similes and metaphors are perfectly good, honest literary devices. Just don't overdo them. And also be sure to create some of your own. Be original but make sure people understand your allusions. Four or five each is plenty for a novel. You don't want readers to think that you are a Raymond Chandler copycat.

4.8 Epigrams & Aphorisms (short witty sayings)

Quick, pithy sayings can add tremendously to the tone, characterization, and originality in your novel. If you can't think of any yourself, then be sure to credit the originator (see 3.15).

"There are two types of statistics: Those you look up, and those you make up."
—Rex Stout

"Better to be without sense than misapply it."
—Jane Austen

"Only cream and bastards rise to the top."
—Ross Macdonald

4.9 Sex
If sex is important to the plot or characterization, then use it. If it is not, then don't.

4.10 Violence
If violence is important to the plot, then use it. If it is not, then don't.

4.11 Vulgarity
If vulgarity is important to character development or tone, then use it. If it is not, then don't.

4.12 Romance
If romance is important to character development or the plot, then use it. If it is not, then don't. Be sure you understand the fundamental difference between the genres (read the established authors). Keep in mind that many readers (and editors) expect some romance in mystery novels. Moreover, "romance" sells. In fact, romance novels represent 40% of all fiction sales.

4.13 Water

The use of rivers, streams, and oceans can enhance a setting and sometimes intensify the action in your story. Create your own lake or pond. Give it a name readers will never forget.

4.14 Birds and Animals

Knowledge of birds and their habits can be interesting to readers. Hobbies and special knowledge will enhance and add believability to your characters. But write what you know about. Don't introduce flocks of northern bluebirds chilling out with South Atlantic penguins. In Tapply's *Cutter's Run*, his knowledge of beavers proves quite valuable not just for the novel's setting, but for helping to solve the mystery.

4.15 Touches

A reader will remember good but incidental *touches* to a story. An excellent example is the scene in *The French Connection* when Popeye Doyle is staked out in the freezing New York winter miserably munching a cold slice of pizza while the bad guy is inside a cozy restaurant spooning warm lobster bisque with a silver spoon. This is where you must recall your own experiences or rely on your own keen perceptions of the human experience to show how such trifling incidents relate to the average person. Incidentally, Robin Moore told me that Eddie Eagan, the real-life detective from whom Popeye Doyle was created, really did have to stand out in the cold as depicted in the movie.

4.16 Police Procedure

If you are going to write a police procedural then make sure you know exactly how police procedure works. Ed McBain would often drive around with on-duty cops and so did Robin Moore when writing *The French Connection*. Robin told me that he wanted to write like a cop, so he lived like one.

4.17 Human Fetishes

People often do strange things that reflect personality traits. Share these odd habits with your reader. Is a particular character always wiping, quoting, cleaning, eating, rubbing, turning wedding band, clicking pen, smiling, nervously laughing, adjusting bra, adjusting boxer shorts, talking about sex/anti-sex, putting a hand through hair, twirling jewelry, talking about money, conscious of breath, cooking, playing with TV clicker, juggling car keys?

Does the bad guy's fetish or unusual habits eventually betray him and give him away?

4.18 Odor/Smell

Your sleuth ought to be aware of smells and odors. A basic knowledge of perfumes, colognes, and the stench of a corpse is impressive. Smells and odors associated with buildings and regions are also effective (the Chicago stockyards, for instance, in mid-August).

4.19 Logic

Don't think you can fool the reader. Always be logical. Have your sleuth verbalize the possible solutions for the reader, as if seeking the reader's assistance for solving the puzzle. This is a also great way to *recap* what has gone on in the "investigation." Sometimes a skillful writer can introduce a new element during this interlude that "muddies" the waters and serves to further confuse the reader. Your sleuth might be saying, "Mary Jane was the only one with the opportunity to kill Biff, but she had no motive. Where am I going wrong? I just can't figure this thing out." There are two basic types of reasoning:

> *Deduction*: Reasoning from known facts or general principles to a logical conclusion (*Webster's New World Dictionary,* 1976).
> *Example:* "All whales are mammals. Moby Dick is a whale. Therefore, Moby Dick is a mammal."

> *Induction:* Reasoning from *particular* facts to a general conclusion (*Webster's,* 1976).
> *Example*: "I know Matlock likes hotdogs. Maybe I'll find him at Nathan's hotdog stand."

Tip: Think of induction as a "hunch." Sometimes a hunch pays off, sometimes it does not.

Tip: Remember the master, Sherlock Holmes, who reasoned, "Eliminate all other factors, and the one which remains must be the truth," (*The Sign of the Four*) and "… when you have excluded the impossible, whatever remains, however improbable, must be the truth ("The Adventure of the Blanched Soldier").

4.20 Foreign Language Usage

Readers generally enjoy mainstream foreign language phrases.

> *Coup de grâce:* "The final blow. The killing stroke"
> *Coup de main:* "A surprise attack"
> *Sub rosa:* "Under the rose—secretly, privately
> *Que pasa:* What's up?
> *Ça va:* What's up?
> *Hasta la vista, baby!*

4.21 Family Traditions

Do your characters have any unique family or ethnic traditions? This can help make reading a mystery educational and can help make your characters round, not flat.

4.22 Symbolism

Some experts, Lady Mary Stewart among them, frown at symbolism, but it sometimes makes for a good touch.

In the opening of Raymond Chandler's *The Big Sleep*, the image of a knight is depicted on a broad, stained-glass panel over the entrance of the Sternwood's main hallway. The knight is attempting to free a nude woman tied to a tree and he's "not getting anywhere." The knight is merely an image and therefore, unable to complete his task. He can never rescue her. Philip Marlowe, the protagonist, is the corporeal embodiment of the determined knight. Despite Marlowe's efforts to make everything all right with the world and to transcend the divide among classes, nothing will ever change. Like the knight he can never quit, but he will always be "fiddling with the knots" and "not getting anywhere."

As George V. Higgins' *The Friends of Eddie Coyle* begins, hoodlum Jackie Brown is introduced as being twenty-six and having no expression on his face. In the last chapter, as Brown awaits trial for his crimes, he is again described as having no expression on his face and the only thing that has changed about him is his age. He is now twenty-seven. Brown is the same individual he was at the beginning the story. He has learned nothing and cares about nothing. In jail or out of jail he will be a prisoner of his own indifference and likewise the prosecutors and defense attorneys around him care little about his fate or his crimes. The individuals in the system will not change and therefore, the system won't—just its players.

At the end of Rex Stout's *A Family Affair* (the last Wolfe story written by Stout) the front door of Nero Wolfe's brownstone is shattered, reminding Nero Wolfe that our responsibilities carry beyond our own threshold.

If symbolism isn't overdone or thrown in the reader's face, then it can add wonderful touches, perhaps heighten suspense or bolster characterization.

4.23 Alcohol/Drugs
Is your protagonist a recovering alcoholic? Did he

experiment with drugs? In Nam, maybe? Temptation can make for good sub-plot or additional story lines, but does suggest a more serious tone for your novel. Sherlock Holmes is a cocaine addict in the early stories and often suffers from depression. Philip Marlowe is a heavy drinker and Robert Parker's Jesse Stone is a functional alcoholic.

4.24 Dichotomy

Do any of your characters have conflicting personalities? In Chapter One for example, Joe praises Michael Collins for liberating Ireland, then in a later chapter calls someone an Irish bum and refuses to see the contradiction.

4.25 Humor

Humor can add tremendously to your story. And remember that editors and agents are human. Get them laughing and they may read on. When asked what mysteries lacked most, Rex Stout said, "Humor!"

A good literary device might be to begin a chapter with the opening of a joke. Then the teller of the joke gets sidetracked; the phone rings, he has to re-set the fussy old temperamental dishwasher, the police arrive, a rock comes through the window, the baby cries, between taking pitches in a batting cage, etc. But before the chapter closes, the teller of the joke finally gets to deliver the punch line. Now you've had your reader hooked for a whole chapter or major scene. The reader just had to know "How many sea turtles it takes to replace a light bulb."

4.26 Occupations

You may opt to give your characters creative, unusual jobs, but jobs that you know something about. Maybe a secondary character works at a car wash because that's where you worked your junior year in high school. This is a good time to list all the odd jobs you've ever had and try to visualize the particulars of that job. You'll need just enough to give the reader a sense of what it is like to work at a fishing pier, as a bartender, stone mason, waitress, or receptionist. Write down the things you used to do and say in these jobs. If you have never been a supreme court justice, you will have to do some research, but even if you sit in district court for a couple of hours, you will get an idea of how a judge really operates. You will also pick up some good dialogue.

4.27 Adverbs

Avoid them when possible. They are lazy words. Words like "very" and "slowly" indicate a lack of creativity. Find better ways to express your ideas and characters.

Example 1 (weak adverbs)
> She walked into the room and made her way over to me slowly after pouring herself a Scotch. I was very pleased with how she looked.

Example 2 (no adverbs)
> She entered the room and took a familiar path to the drink service. Scotch was her

pleasure. Stupid me. I'd left my kilt at the cleaners. Second time this month.

4.28 Special Talent
Maybe your sleuth has some special talent: explosives expert, former big rig driver, trial attorney, computer tech, wine and cheese connoisseur, gun expert, marksman, professor of American history, hot dog junkie, geology buff, angler, or biker. Somehow this talent is going to play into the plot and perhaps even the resolution of the conflict.

4.29 Get a Hobby
Characters who plant flowers or raise vegetable gardens can be interesting. Rex Stout's Nero Wolfe occupies his spare time tending to his orchids, and Miss Marple can often be found tending to her English garden. Robert Parker's Spenser knows his beer.

In the very successful television series "Matlock" (played by Andy Griffith), Matlock is always questing the perfect hot dog. This great little touch not only makes for subtle humor, but it also humanizes Matlock. Holmes plays the violin. Agatha Christie's Poroit is always tending to his mustache and praising anything Belgian.

4.30 On the Road Again
You won't be stopped at a red light in Nantucket because they don't have any. If you have your sleuth blasting through New York City and she always finds

a parking space and never runs into a STOP sign, then you will lose reader confidence. Take a ride through the setting you choose and note the traffic signals. Also note how long it takes you to get from point A to point B. Rex Stout's Archie Goodwin often took cabs because he lived in New York City.

Robin Moore told me that he took painstaking measures to make sure he had all the New York City streets correct in *The French Connection*, making sure, for example, that he didn't have cars traveling the wrong way down a one way street. However, when the movie came out, some streets changed to become one way and one ways became two way streets. People actually wrote to him pointing out these "inaccuracies." Ahh, the life of a writer. We can never please everyone, so get used to it now.

4.31 Lighting & Darkness
Light and darkness can contribute greatly to the tone of your story. These devices can also help the reader visualize a room or setting and can also suggest danger or safety.

4.32 Gangster vs. Cozy vs. Hardboiled
What kind of mystery will you write? Philip Marlowe or Miss Marple? Beginning writers will enjoy the greatest satisfaction by selecting the type of novel they most enjoy reading. Be sure to "visit" as many stories as possible because even in a cozy mystery you can still have a hard-boiled character and vice-versa.

4.33 Clichés

Avoid them. Never use phrases like "He bled like a stuck pig" or "She stuck out like a sore thumb." This tells editors, agents, and readers that you are an amateur and that you are lazy or, worse, not creative. Create your own phrases (don't be afraid of incongruity and/or humor) like, "She stuck out like a chain saw in a plastic surgeon's office."

4.34 Irony

Irony is a great touch in mystery stories.

Examples:

A character states how much he loves his pig and then casually remarks that Mr. Pig will be Christmas dinner. Another character pays more attention to his pet salamander than the wife he intends to kill. And in the end, through some plot manipulations, it is his love for his salamander that is his ultimate undoing.

Consider a greedy mine owner who spends his whole life cheating small miners out of their claims. In the end, while inspecting a mine which he's schemed from another poor miner, he is crushed to death when the mine collapses.

CHAPTER FIVE

Clues
& Making Tracks

5.1 Hiding Clues

Laying out clues for the reader is one of the corner-
stones of good mystery writing. The reader must
know everything the sleuth knows. Cheat readers and
you have lost them forever. So how do you provide
clues and still maintain the puzzle until the very end?
You must learn "the clue shell game." Here are some
examples of how you can play this game.

In lists. "Hide" clues in lists. The sleuth empties a
   purse and finds several seemingly useless items
   which he itemizes for the reader. Or the sleuth
   videotapes an office interior and then describes
   the items on the videotape. Later, it is revealed
   that the seemingly "unimportant" water bubbler
   is actually a clue.

Misinterpretation. Clues are hidden in circumstances involving "cause and effect." For example: A woman comes home to find her husband digging in the garden. That night he complains about a splinter in his hand and she assumes that this was a result of his gardening activities. Earlier, however, readers learned that a cat burglar is on the prowl and authorities believe he is gaining entry by using a wooden ladder. Now it is up to the reader to make the connection.

Humor. A clue is revealed when a character in the story passes something off as a joke but the reader is too busy laughing to take note. For example: Someone in a bar makes a quip about so-and-so being a cheapskate. The victim was murdered while clipping coupons and when the sleuth pieces the coupon circular back together, she notices one coupon is missing. Was the killer so cheap that he actually couldn't resist taking the coupon with him?

Confusion/Meaning. In this instance, an obvious clue is shared with the reader but the significance of the clue is totally unknown. For example, rose petals and a small bottle of iodine are left at a series of murder scenes. Why is the culprit doing this and what is he trying to tell us?

Finally, maybe you don't *hide* the clue at all. Perhaps you'll use the "dying clue device." Before the victim dies, she manages to stick a pencil into a fresh angel food cake. What is she trying to tell us? How does the victim's final, desperate act help your sleuth divulge who the killer is? We don't know just yet, but one thing is for sure: Your sleuth has only 24 hours to find out or else so-and-so will be executed!

5.2 Antagonist vs. Protagonist

Make the story personal. Why does the protagonist want to catch the antagonist so badly? Why is your sleuth so dedicated to the cause? Is it purely the quest for justice or is the antagonist out to get your sleuth specifically? Did the bad guy kill someone your sleuth knows or loves? Did the bad guy slip through your sleuth's hands years before? Or, perhaps the bad guy will kill again and only *your sleuth* can stop him. There should be a more important motive than just the simple quest for truth (although that is a big part of the story). For some compelling reason, your sleuth *must* catch the bad guy.

5.3 Justice

There ought to be some. If the bad guy gets away and lives happily ever after, then you have written a stinker. For the purposes of realism, you may be able to pull this off, but even if the bad guy does get away, the reader should be left with the feeling that the bad guy will have a terrible, lonely, guilty life, and perhaps will live in squalor and on the run from the cops. Think of divine justice — time wounds all heels.

5.4 Choose Your Weapons

Like Luke Skywalker, choose and use your weapons wisely. Good weapons include guns, clubs, knives, and poison.

Make the murder weapon *interesting*. If the victim is going to be clubbed to death then a fireplace poker or tree branch is boring. Use something like a bust of John F. Kennedy or a hatchet that was on display at a Lizzie Borden exhibit or an old Indian club once used by Teddy Roosevelt. If the victim is to be stabbed, try using a scrimshaw whale's tooth that, according to local folklore, was once owned by Herman Melville.

Remember that the *manner* in which a victim is murdered can create action and tension. The actual method of killing may reflect the cruel nature and depraved mental state of the perpetrator — someone who enjoys his work. Therefore, we become all the more anxious for our sleuth to catch the bad guy.

Where your victim is killed can also create suspense. In Katherine Hall Page's first book, *The Body in the Belfry* (which won the Agatha Award), a victim is found in the same belfry once used to call the Lexington Minutemen to arms and where the "shot heard 'round the world" was fired.

Your sleuth's weapon of choice is also important. Dirty Harry just wouldn't be "Dirty Harry" without his .44 magnum. Dr. Watson often carries his service revolver. And Miss Marple's weapon of choice? Her mind!

5.5 Feel Your Weapons

Master story teller Helen McCloy beat a watermelon "to death" with a baseball bat just to experience what it felt like to crush and bash in a skull and to test splatter marks.

When training to learn how to inject a needle, nurses will practice on an orange, which has about the same resistance as human skin. Get a feel for things like this.

If the proper and legal circumstances present themselves, fire a gun at a shooting range with the assistance of an expert. I did this and was amazed at how difficult it is to hit a target. Knowing that a cop doesn't have time to install earplugs during a shootout, I also removed my earplugs just to see what actual gunfire really sounds like. I thought my eardrums were going to explode.

5.6 Suicide

The solution to a puzzle should *never* be that no one committed the crime. The reader will feel cheated and will probably want to strap you to the nearest railroad track if it turns out that the victim killed himself.

5.7 Supernatural

The solution to a puzzle should *never* be that the Ghost of Christmas Past committed the crime. Ahh, the victim was killed by the ghost of Blackbeard the Pirate. The reader will feel cheated. If you want to write a ghost story, then write a ghost story.

5.8 Fair Play

Always engage in fair play with your readers. Give them all the clues your sleuth has. If you don't, then you will lose reader confidence.

5.9 Accuracy

Be accurate. A woman will not get shot in the Adam's apple because women do not have Adam's apples. There may be a woman somewhere in the world with an Adam's apple, and if there is and you are determined to make this woman a character, then your reader should know that she is a *woman* with an Adam's apple. Every so often you hear about someone who was born with his heart on his right side instead of his left. If one of your characters has such a characteristic, then let the reader know.

5.10 Description

Remember that your story is competing with computer games, TiVo, cell phones, the internet, cable TV, etc. Be *brief* in descriptive passages and make sure they don't get in the way of either plot or action. One way to introduce description is through quick, punchy dialogue.

"Man, you've put on some poundage, Joe." A wan smile crossed Betty's face.

"Four kids, a wife who's allergic to the stove, and twelve hours a day strapped in this thing!" Joe banged the palms of his hands on the arms of his office chair. "Who the hell did you expect — Mel Gibson?!"

Betty looked around the office. "No. I always expected you'd end up something like this."

With this brief exchange, the reader quickly learns that Joe is middle-aged, overweight, has a tough family life, and a job he probably doesn't like, that life seems to be passing him by and he feels trapped. At the same time, the reader learns that Betty has managed to keep her girlish figure (otherwise she wouldn't be poking fun at Joe's weight) and she's not surprised that Joe is in his current "state." And who is Betty? She's someone Joe hasn't seen for a while. It doesn't require page after page of narrative detailing, "Who is Joe? Why is he unhappy? And where does Betty fit in?" The reader can determine these things immediately through some simple dialogue. We also notice that Betty has a way of getting under Joe's collar. The last thing he wants is for her to see him this way and she knows it. And she knows that he knows it. And he knows that she knows it. Poor Joe.

Tip: Note the use of punctuation in this dialogue. *Before* "Mel Gibson" there is a dash, suggesting a short pause for the speaker. And *after* the sentence there is both a question mark and exclamation point which, together, suggest a rhetorical and frustrated question. The punctuation used here helps to avoid annoying tag lines which tend to slow down the pace and action, such as, "Joe said, rhetorically."

CHAPTER SIX

Character Development

When I set out to become a serious writer, I asked Boston writer Kelly Lawrence, author of the excellent hard-boiled novel *The Gone Shots*, if he had any tips for me. He said that when he was starting out, he asked Helen McCloy—the mother of the psychological thriller—what advice she might offer. She told him that the most important thing was to know your character. I have found this to be excellent advice. Know *who* your main character is as best you can. The more you know about him, the more real he becomes. Readers must believe in your sleuth and they will only believe if you do. If you don't know who your character is, no one else will either. This does not mean that you need to know everything there is to know about your sleuth. Your sleuth's character will grow with each story and you will learn new things about her. And by having some surprises left, you will be less apt to "contrive" your character. In my father's book, *Royal Decree*, which included his most memorable conversations with Rex Stout, Stout contends that, "A character who is thought out is not born, he or she is contrived. A born character is round, a thought-out character is flat."

6.1 Amateur vs. Professional Sleuth

What kind of sleuth do you have here? Professional or amateur? Do you have a "Miss Marple" who always seems to stumble upon murder in the English garden or a "Sam Spade" who is paid to crack murder cases? Is your sleuth a cop? A retired cop who still wants to fight crime?

Tip: Think very carefully about your sleuth choice. *Why* your sleuth solves murders and how he gets dragged into these cases just may be the most important decision you make concerning your character's development. Your character should be someone you want to hang out with for the rest of your life because, as bizarre as it sounds, characters do become real. You are choosing a life-long mate here, so don't create a jackass.

6.2 Names

Your sleuth's name and your characters' names are essential. Put great thought into these names because, once your books are published, you are stuck with them and so is the rest of the world. Give your sleuth a name that makes him or her distinctive, something that readers will remember forever and maybe even relate to.

6.3 Hobbies

What hobbies will your sleuth have? Make your sleuth interesting. Does she make honey, play pool, tend orchids like Nero Wolfe, jog, make jams, make cribbage boards, play the tuba, write software? Is he an accomplished sailor? How might her hobby save the day/help solve the crime? How does it help him think? Sherlock Holmes plays the violin sometimes while pondering clues. Robert Parker's sleuth, Spenser, carves wood. (*See also* Chapter 4.29)

6.4 Superiority

Consider creating a colorful but haughty character; a snob, for instance, who thinks that the masses are asses. Winthorp, while petting his cat (which wears a diamond-studded collar), explains to your sleuth that starvation is a fact of life and that there will always be murder. But what he can't tolerate is how he can't find a servant who can serve piping hot tea properly.

6.5 Psychology of the Criminal Mind

The legal term *mens rea* is Latin for criminal intent (malice). Crimes of *intent* include murder, stealing, burglary, rape, blackmail, arson, assault and battery, and drug trafficking. Crimes that don't require intent are crimes such as speeding, double-parking, operating a motor vehicle while under the influence of alcohol, etc. These crimes are known as *mal prohibitum* and are bad simply because the legislature says they are bad and has enumerated so in a statute.

Is your sleuth into the psychology of the criminal mind? Robert Parker's Spenser has a girlfriend, Susan Silverman, who is a psychiatrist. Spenser often consults with her to learn about the "whys" of crime. Why would a criminal behave a certain way? James M. Cain also does this very well as does Georges Simenon's Inspector Maigret.

6.6 Marriage vs. Divorce

Is your sleuth married? Single? Divorced? Dating? Not ready to date? Marital status may dictate much of your sleuth's personality. William Tapply once wrote that he wanted Brady Coyne to be divorced so that Brady could date. This enhances the story lines because Brady has two sons from his marriage. Hence, we have the relationship between a divorced father and his two sons as well as his former wife — and to top it off, we have a murder or two to solve here!

But don't kill off the spouse idea too quickly! Georges Simenon's character, Inspector Maigret has a wonderful wife, and where would Columbo be without his famous line, "You know, I was talkin' to the Mrs. about this case, and she thinks …" Get to know Nick and Nora Charles, the famous detective team in Dashiell Hammett's *The Thin Man*. Think of all the romance you could include!

6.7 Office & Chair

Your sleuth's office and office chair can be very important. It is his comfort zone. Put great thought into where you want your sleuth to hang out a shingle. How is the office decorated? Is there a motif? Does the office reflect nautical, political, sports, classic film interests or is it indicative of intellectual pursuits such as a library? If there no motif at all, then what would this say about your sleuth? Think of Nero Wolfe's New York office or Spenser's office overlooking Boston, or Miss Marple's bucolic cottage.

6.8   Hats

Hats are not worn as much as in times past, but the type of hat one wears can say much about his or her nature: Red Sox, Yankees, Cubs baseball caps, Scottish tam, French beret, etc.

Tip: Try putting a typical man's cap on a woman. Think of a woman wearing an Orange County Chopper cap or a Red Man Chewing Tobacco cap. What does this say about her other than just being a motorcycle or chewing tobacco fan? Simply by switching caps, you may have just invented a wonderful character.

6.9   Veteran Status

Today, women can be veterans. This may be an interesting characteristic of a main or even secondary character. A veteran suggests someone who is worldly, who has seen more than his or her share of grief, joy, and camaraderie. Someone who has seen the best and worst in people. A veteran will usually have a special knowledge of weaponry, firearms, and military slang.

6.10 The Victim

While not *necessarily* sympathetic you should make the victim interesting. If a businessman is found dead, slumped over his office desk, this may be suspenseful, but it is somewhat anemic. Imagine now that the businessman is Nelson Rockefeller and a snooping reporter believes that he actually died somewhere else and that the body was just moved to his office. (As was allegedly the case.)

Tip: Make the victim someone readers care about so they'll want to catch the bad guy as much as your sleuth does. Conversely, you could make the victim someone readers hate. This will create more suspects and enhance your puzzle.

CHAPTER SEVEN

Plot Pourri

7.1 Plotting – Action and Reaction

Your tenth-grade chemistry teacher was correct: for every ACTION there is a REACTION. The mystery plot is no exception. In a mystery story certain crimes can lead to murder. These include (but are not limited to) white-collar crimes, kidnappings, heists, blackmail, etc. These are "set-up crimes" that lead to murder.

There is an ACTION (a set-up crime) and, *as a direct result,* there is REACTION (murder). There must be an action and reaction in your mystery plot. The PLOT is the cornerstone of the novel and it becomes a building when you introduce characters who *create action* and are ultimately *affected* by this action. (*See also*: 1.9 Hitchcock and the McGuffin.)

Your story must have the following elements:
- a victim
- a murderer (antagonist)

- a motive for killing the victim
- a sleuth (protagonist)
- a solution

The three most common *motives* for committing murder are:
- Money
- Power
- Love

Look for the *action* and *reaction* in the following examples. I did the first one for you and note that "action" does not always precede "reaction."

> "I will murder so-and-so (*reaction*), because she will divulge our affair (*action*) and I will lose my congressional seat."

> "If I kill so-and-so, I will win the congressional seat and then be powerful."

> "If I kill so-and-so, I will have all the money."

> "I have to kill so-and-so because he found out I stole the money."

> "Once so-and-so is out of the way, I can marry Matilda."

> "She slept with so-and-so. Now I must kill them both."

"He made me give up my baby for adoption.
I must kill him, because I loved my baby."

7.2   Structuring the Plot

Agatha Award-nominated author and UCLA instructor Kris Neri (*Never Say Die*) offers this invaluable advice concerning story structure:

Before I apply my story to the 3-act structure, I look at the story elements from three different angles: 1) *back story* — I separate out the elements that lead up to the crime, just to be sure I don't give too much history, which can slow down the narrative flow, and so I use it to hook the reader; 2) *the villain's story* — I work out the villain's behind-the-scenes actions: how he carries out the crime, how he establishes his alibi, how he casts doubt on someone else, etc; by working through it before I write the book, I'm sure there won't be any holes; and 3) *the story I'll write for the reader* — only after I separate out the back story, and work through the crime as it's carried out from the villain's perspective, do I tackle the book's story line, which is from the protagonist's perspective.

7.3   Theme

Veteran editor and author Paula Munier offers this on literary *theme:*

If plot is the bones of a book and character its brain, then theme is its heart. Think of *To Kill a Mockingbird*, in which Harper Lee asks the question: "Are people basically good or evil?"

That theme echoes through every aspect of the story, through the plot, the characters, the setting itself. It's what makes this crime novel one of the masterpieces of American literature.

How you handle a *theme* such as this one can make the difference between good and great storytelling and occasionally permits a writer to transcend the *genre* altogether. Common themes include "the mystery of death," "the uncertainty of the future," and "the impetuousness of youth."

James M. Cain famously weaves "love vs. lust" and "friendship vs. betrayal" as the twin themes in *Double Indemnity*.

Examine how successful writers use literary theme in their stories. Keep in mind that theme does not always have to be serious. Emma Lathen wrote a light-hearted series around an unlikely protagonist, Wall Street banker John Putnam Thatcher of Sloan Guaranty Trust. In *Accounting for Murder* for example, the victim is strangled with the cord to his adding machine. The themes of Wall Street finance, business and attendant intrigues are crucial to both crimes and solutions in this best-selling collection.

7.4 Sample Outline Template for Plotting

ACTION (crime)
   Bob tries to blackmail Fred for money.

REACTION (plot)
   Fred is not intimidated by Bob's threat of blackmail and plans to report Bob to the police. Bob
   then murders Fred because if word gets out that
   Bob is a blackmailer, Bob will lose his position as
   a stockbroker and be ruined.

BACK STORY
   Your Sleuth served in the Gulf War with Bob, and
   Bob saved his life. Fred is your *Sleuth's boyhood
   friend.*

SLEUTH
   Your Sleuth is determined to avenge the death of
   his boyhood friend. But when the net closes in on
   Bob, Sleuth has to choose between turning in the
   comrade who saved his life and avenging the
   murder of his boyhood friend.

SETTING
   New York City (primary setting); Chicago;
   Hanscom Air Force Base, Massachusetts.

WEAPON
   The same knife Bob used to save Sleuth in Gulf
   War, (but the actual knife *is not disclosed* until the
   climactic scene).

NARRATION
First-Person (POV)

TIME ELEMENT
Sleuth has been called back into the military and scheduled to ship out in three days. He must solve the crime before shipping out because he doesn't know when he'll be back or even if he'll be back. For some reason, the police just don't seem to care about Fred's murder, so it's up to your Sleuth to solve the crime on his own.

SUSPECTS
A, B, and C all have strong links to Fred and have motive to kill him. For some reason, A and C lie about their alibis. B has no verifiable alibi.

SECONDARY AND TERTIARY CHARACTERS
Sleuth's girlfriend who helps him solve cases; friend from the DA's office who feeds him bits of information; police detective who dislikes Sleuth; local bartender full of advice; newspaper salesman Sleuth always trades quips with; pet dog.

ADDITIONAL STORYLINE (Sub-plots)
Sleuth is spending last few days solving murder instead of spending them with girlfriend. Tension builds. Will she be here when he gets back? Will she take care of his dog *while he is gone?*

Experiment with this and create additional storylines to enhance the plot, detection, and resolution.

7.5 Sample Background Story Lines

Your protagonist is trying to learn how to cook, or quit booze or cigarettes, or go on a diet and everywhere she goes her favorite meals are being served. Her son is sick, a spouse may be cheating, or maybe your sleuth is trying to guess the number one song on the Memorial Holiday Weekend 100-Best-Songs Countdown. Remember that this last example will confine your action to one weekend, so the time element will add suspense and tension. (And yes, the reader will want to know what the number one song is, too.)

7.6 The Big "Why"

Why does so-and-so wipe caramel and catsup onto a ten-pound dumbbell and then carefully place it in a shoebox along with a gun? *Why* does he stealthily place the shoebox in his car trunk? (Or if you are in Great Britain, in the boot.) A perfect example of a "Big Why" mystery is Gregory Mcdonald's *Fletch*—why does a seemingly healthy and successful businessman want Fletch to murder him? In *The Maltese Falcon,* why is everyone after the "black bird"? In James Patterson's *4th of July,* why is the adversary willing to do *anything* to conceal the motive behind the murders?

Maybe your big "Why" could be one like this: Why is a beautiful woman being chased through the woods by an individual in a clown suit holding a lion trainer's whip?

7.7 Lying

What are the reasons that all six suspects must avoid telling the truth? One will be lying because she or he committed the murder. The others, however, may have perfectly understandable motives for lying. So-and-so is having an affair, so he claims that he was at work while the murder was committed, when in actuality he was at the Ritz with his mistress. Mrs. Jones can't say that she was at Town Hall when the murder was committed, so she says that she was at home. She lies because she had business to complete concerning her adopted daughter who does not know yet that she is adopted. Lying makes suspects appear "guilty" and it will be up to your sleuth to uncover the lies and the reasons behind them. This adds confusion to the puzzle and is also a good source for developing additional storylines.

7.8 Red Herring

A red herring is a device writers use to throw readers off the "scent." The source probably comes from fox hunters who manage to draw off the hounds by dragging a red herring across their path. Red herrings can add suspense to your story and include (but are not limited to) elements such as a false suspect, a false clue, a confusing clue, or the sleuth's failure to ask a crucial question.

7.9 Cigarettes & Lipstick

If your sleuth solves a crime because he notes that the cigarette was smoked by a woman since it has lipstick on the filter, then you ought to be in the cosmetic business, not the mystery writing business.

7.10 Writers Groups

Should you join one? Yes. A writers group can offer great feedback on what you have written and it will likely be your first opportunity to see how the "public" views your work. A good and diverse group can help you conquer plot snares and writer's block, develop dialogue, support character development and, among other things, give you different perspectives into the literary world and beyond. If you join a writers group, consider *when* you would like to join. You may want to join while your manuscript is a work in progress or you may wish to wait until you have completed your first draft. Your local library or local Mystery Writers of America chapter may be able to help you find a writers group or provide the opportunity to meet other authors who wish to form a group.

7.11 Blank Outline Template

Create your own thumbnail plot by using the following elements as illustrated earlier in Section 7.4.

Action (crime)
Reaction (plot)
Sleuth
Back Story
Setting
Weapon
Narrator
Time Element

Suspects
Secondary and Tertiary Characters
Additional Storyline(s)/Sub-plots

FINAL WORD

Finding a literary agent and marketing your novel is a whole new subject and is a battle for another day. ABOVE ALL ELSE, *the most important thing for you to do is to write your mystery.* If, however, you do wish to land an agent and sell your book, then make your book marketable. When asked what were the five factors most likely to interest him in a new client's work, literary agent Dominick Abel—one of the most respected literary agents in the business—responded, "Voice. Voice. Voice. Voice. Recommendations from respected persons unrelated to the author." (June/July 2004 "3rd Degree Newsletter," Mystery Writers of America.)

I have found most established writers to be more than willing to help new writers of merit. If you find your voice, you will earn recommendations from established authors, but the rest is up to you. You must have a voice. Keep writing and reading and you will find it. The key is not to give up. Good luck and get to work! Read anything you can get your hands on— even cereal boxes.

A great book for locating a reputable agent is *The Writer's Market* and, best of all, it can probably be found in your local library. Be leery of agents who charge a fee for representing your work or recommend a "book doctor" you will have to pay for "revising" your manuscript. (A good writers group will help you screen most issues you have with your manuscript anyway.) Agents should work on a commission and get paid only when your book sells.

FINAL TIPS
Read. Read. Read.

If an established author, editor, or agent *does* help you, send a "thank-you" note. If *no* help was provided, send a "thank-you" note anyway. Always be professional.

And remember—when you do get published, *real* friends *buy* your book and don't expect a free copy.

NOTES:

_____

_____

_____

_____

_____

IMPORTANT ADDRESSES

Mystery Writers of America, Inc.
17 E. 47th St. 6th Floor
New York, NY 10017
www.mysterywriters.org

Private Eye Writers of America
P.O. Box 202
Clarksville, MO 63336

Femmes Fatales
P.O Box 1248
Cypress, TX 77410-1248
www.femmesfatalesauthors.com

Sisters in Crime
www.sistersincrime.org

www.ThrillingDetective.com

www.spensersmysterybooks.com

www.katesmysterybooks.com

www.CrimeStalkers.com

www.rockpublishing.com

Conversations About Writers and Writing

Ten Questions for William G. Tapply
An interview by Andrew McAleer
from *Crimestalker Casebook*, Vol. VI, No. 2. August 2004

McAleer: Not too long ago Poisoned Pen Press republished a fine edition of your first "Brady Coyne" novel, *Death at Charity Point* and in your updated Introduction you mention that the first-person narrative is what ultimately introduced you to Brady's voice. James M. Cain took the position that the first-person narrative has a ring of truth to it that the third-person does not. Would you agree with Cain's assessment here?

Tapply: I think an author's choice of point of view is one of the most important writing decisions she can make — and, in my experience, it's rarely given serious thought by beginning writers. POV gives readers a place to stand and eyes and ears for experiencing the events of the story. First-person gives readers a specific person as a guide. Third-person gives them . . . an author. In fact, I stumbled on first-person by trial and error. When I tried it, it sounded right and felt comfortable. This makes sense. The first-person POV gives me a voice, a way of seeing the story's world. And it enables me to present a mystery honestly. With third-person, no matter how well done it is, readers are always aware of The Author out there manipulating things, pulling strings, revealing only what she wants to reveal, dipping into and out of the heads of various characters, sharing and withholding information at will. I think that's what Cain means by third-person lacking the complete honesty that a candid first-person narrator conveys. First-person is a conversation between a trustworthy narrator and trusting reader. It's really a speaking voice, not a written, literary voice.

McAleer: In *Dead Meat* there seems to be a high rate of chewing tobacco usage. As an avid outdoorsman, do you ever take a chaw?

Tapply: I stuffed a chaw into my cheek once. Chewed for about a minute, gagged, and spit it out. Never again. In the out of doors, tobacco addicts sometimes can't smoke because of the fear of forest fires, so they chew. I smoked cigarettes for close to 35 years. Quit three months ago.

McAleer: How would you rate the Nero Wolfe stories?

Tapply: I like them enormously. Archie, the first-person narrator, is actually one of my favorite mystery characters. Subconsciously, probably, he's a model for Brady Coyne, my narrator. I wrote an introduction to a paperback reprint of *The Second Confession.* Your father and my friend John McAleer wrote the definitive biography of Rex Stout. I enjoyed it tremendously.

McAleer: Your knowledge of the day-to-day workings of a small law practice seems as authentic as my granddaddy's old leatherback editions on Negotiable Instruments. As a lawyer in private practice I know. Did you ever work in a law firm?

Tapply: Never. I just made it all up based on casual conversations with lawyer friends of mine plus how I imagined it might be. When the books started coming out, I got a lot of good feedback from practicing attorneys telling me that finally somebody got the day-to-day inner workings of a small law practice right.

McAleer: Brady hangs his shingle right in Proper Boston. Was there a special reason why you chose the Boston setting?

Tapply: Boston is hardly proper, of course, although that is one of its delicious contradictions. When I began writing, I'd lived in eastern Massachusetts all my life, and Boston was the only city I knew well enough to write about. I make up characters, but most of my setting material is authentic. I could've put Brady in a suburb, but that seemed to me to limit my possibilities. I think of my novels as New England stories, not Boston stories. But still, Boston is a wonderfully diverse city ethnically, socially, economically, politically, even geographically, where anything can happen.

McAleer: What might Brady's reaction be if his secretary, Julie, took a week's vacation and the employment agency sent in Miss Marple as her replacement?

Tapply: Brady would promptly take his own week's vacation. That would be this author's prerogative . . . I never much liked Miss Marple. In one early book Julie took a maternity leave, and Brady took on a clerk named Xerxes Garret. Zerk became an ongoing character in my stories.

McAleer: Your better half, Vicki Stiefel recently published a top-notch Boston-based suspense novel, *Body Parts*. Can fans expect another soon?

Tapply: Oh, yes. We're thrilled that her publisher has made an offer for her second novel. She is almost done with it. Right now its title is *The Dead Stone* and they want to bring it out in March 2005. (Editor's note: *The Dead Stone* is now available.)

McAleer: Have you ever read the Mr. Tutt stories by Arthur Train [1875–1945]?

Tapply: No. There are a lot I haven't read, I'm afraid. On the other hand, there's a lot I have read, too. If you recommend these stories, I will check them out.

McAleer: You knew George V. Higgins and in *The Vulgar Boatman* you mention his first novel, *The Friends of Eddie Coyle*. Can we gather from this that you have an appreciation for his work?

Tapply: Absolutely. George created terrific Boston characters, and he wrote the best dialogue ever. *Eddie Coyle* was a great book — and a great movie, too. But I liked all George's stories. I'm sure I've read all of them at least once.

McAleer: There might not be any writer in the crime fiction genre today who knows his restaurants better than you. Any truth to the rumor that you might be the Phantom Gourmet?

Tapply: I better not answer this question . . .

McAleer: Thanks, Bill. Whomever you are.

Ten Questions for Robert B. Parker

An Interview with Andrew McAleer

from *Crimestalker Casebook,* Vol. VIII, No. 1, April 2006

McAleer: Your "Jesse Stone" novels and movie series are a real hit. Tom Selleck is not only staring in the role as Jesse, but he is doing some of the screenplay work as well. Does Selleck ever consult you on what Jesse might do or not do?

Parker: Rarely.

McAleer: Say or not say?

Parker: Rarely.

McAleer: One back story concerning Jesse Stone is that he was a great short stop. If Jesse and Spenser were in their prime, what are the chances that Spenser could slip a single past Jesse?

Parker: Spenser would hit it high and far and it wouldn't be an issue.

McAleer: The "boss of bullet-lettres," George V. Higgins thought very highly of your work. Did you and George ever talk shop?

Parker: George and I were friends, and talked a lot but rarely shop. Most writers talk deals, and book tours, and movie rights, as well as the usual sex and base-ball. But almost never do we talk about writing.

McAleer: Raymond Chandler fans are indebted to you for completing Chandler's unfinished manuscript, *Poodle Springs.* But even though the end result was "McCoy," was stepping into Chandler's shoes a daunting task?

Parker: I don't daunt very much. I was aware that it might be challenging, and I suspected that critics would talk about how presumptuous I was; but I expected to do it well.

McAleer: In *The Godwulf Manuscript,* Spenser consumes five McDonald's hamburgers while on stakeout. How might Susan Silverman react if she got the dope on this?

Parker: With Horror.

McAleer: Not too long ago Helen Hunt thought she might like to bring your Boston-based PI, Sunny Randall to the big screen. Any scoops here?

Parker: Nope, Helen has talked of producing it (though not starring) for TV. We'll see. We do have a deal with Ed Harris to do *Appaloosa.* Ed would direct and play Virgil Cole. Viggo Mortenson is attached to play Hitch, and Diane Lane is attached to play Allie. I've seen the screenplay and its very good. They are working at the moment on financing.

McAleer: If Sherlock Holmes ever came out of retirement as a beekeeper do you think he could ever spread shoe leather with Hawk? (Assume for this question that the Baker Street Irregulars cannot work because of child labor laws and that Watson is lost on the Tube.)

Parker: Hawk would find Sherlock amusing . . . for a junkie.

McAleer: Do you think Spenser could ever cook a meal that might survive Nero Wolfe's scrutiny?

Parker: No.

McAleer: What advice might you give new authors?

Parker: Same old advice, write your novel and send it to someone who can publish it . . . maybe they will.

McAleer: Good advice. We look forward to the movie *Appaloosa.* Great book, too.

Ten Questions for Margaret McLean

An Interview by Andrew McAleer

from *Crimestalker Casebook,* Vol. VIII, No. 2, August 2006

McAleer: In your first book, *Under Oath,* you use an interesting literary device where readers are able to see what goes on in the minds of the jurors during a criminal trial. As a former prosecutor, did you ever have the opportunity to discuss cases with jurors after a trial?

McLean: Yes. On several occasions when I tried drunk driving cases before a jury of six, the judge permitted the attorneys to speak with the jury panel upon agreement of all parties. I was astonished at what factors led to the verdict.

McAleer: In *Under Oath* you use some well-established Bostonian names like Callahan, Twomey, and Kelly. James M. Cain held that name selection is critical in fiction. Would you agree?

McLean: Absolutely. The name has to fit the character. Sometimes it takes weeks to come up with the right name.

McAleer: Fans seem to enjoy your seasoned criminal defense attorney Buddy Clancy in *Under Oath.* Can we expect to see more of Buddy?

McLean: Buddy barges into the courtroom, arriving late for the first day of trial in *Under Fire.* In the last big case, his bus got hit by a Duck Boat. Buddy's excuse this time? "The Big Dig."* Buddy is up to his old tricks again as he defends a first-degree murder and arson case with his young and spunky niece, Sarah Lynch.

McAleer: And his bow tie?

McLean: Buddy has increased his wardrobe of bow ties, including a rat tie when he cross-examines an informant, and an outer space tie to demonstrate "the great beyond" or beyond a reasonable doubt. In fact, people have spotted Buddy in Charlestown walking his dog, Rehnquist, in a matching bow tie.

McAleer: If Perry Mason and Clancy had a cup of joe together what might they discuss?

McLean: The art of cross-examination and all the stories that go with it.

McAleer: Arthur Train [1875–1945], a former New York City prosecutor and creator of Mr. Tutt—a foretaste to Perry Mason—was, like yourself, an author and an attorney. Train once wrote that, to his dismay, his author friends looked at him as a lawyer who wrote and his lawyer friends looked at him as an author who practiced law. Like Train, you are very accomplished in both fields, but do you ever suffer the same "identity crisis" Train did?

McLean: No, I like wearing both hats.

McAleer: Your career as a well-accomplished prosecutor serves you well as a writer, and you have a nice prose style that complements your experiences. Has writing always been a passion?

McLean: Storytelling was a passion long before I learned to write.

McAleer: In *Under Oath* it's apparent that you know your Boston—Charlestown in particular. Did you have to do a lot of research?

McLean: I lived in Charlestown and spent many eve-
   nings at the community garden with the old-tim-
   ers, listening to all the stories . . . and the book was
   born.

McAleer: What book are you reading now?

McLean: *In the Shadow of the Ark*, by Anne Provost. It's
   historical fiction based on the story of Noah's Ark.

McAleer: Can you scoop us on anything about your next
   novel?

McLean: *Under Fire* is an action-packed courtroom
   drama in which a Boston firefighter is shot and killed
   in the line of duty as he rescues a Middle Eastern
   woman and her son from a burning building. The
   woman's store and home are being taken unfairly
   by eminent domain, creating a volatile situation,
   and a motive for arson and murder.

*"The Big Dig" took place primarily in Boston and is one
   of the largest highway improvement projects ever under-
   taken in the United States.

The Writer in Us

John McAleer

John McAleer was the author of over a dozen books including the Edgar Award-winning biography of Rex Stout
(reissued in 2002 as *Rex Stout: A Majesty's Life*) and the
well-received mystery, *Coign of Vantage*. He was nominated for the Pulitzer Prize for his biography of Ralph
Waldo Emerson and was Professor of English at Boston
College for more than half a century. The following ex-
cerpt is from *Royal Decree,* Pontes Press, 1983.

Thirty-three years ago Rex Stout authorized me to
do a book on Nero Wolfe and Archie Goodwin. One
day not long afterward, he told me that some of his
friends wanted him to write an autobiography. He de-
clined emphatically. "Any man who writes an autobiography," he said, "thinks too damn much of himself." When
they saw that he meant it, one of them offered to write
his biography. Rex again said no. "You know me too
well," he explained.

When Rex told me what he had told them I re-
minded him that I didn't fall under that interdict. I had
come onto the scene late in his life. At eighty-two he
was almost twice my age. Could I cast my nets wider to
include him, as well as Wolfe and Archie, in the book I
had underway? Rex never hesitated for an instant. "In a
book about Nero Wolfe and Archie Goodwin," he said,
"I'd just be a hanger-on; in one about me they'll have to
stand till I sit. I like that. You've got yourself a deal."

The next seven years were busy ones. I made frequent visits to Connecticut, to High Meadow—the

majestic house, set in the midst of eighteen acres, which he designed, built and landscaped, with his own hands, at a thousand foot elevation, in 1930—where I taped the miles of conversation that flowed between us. Sometimes we talked from dawn to dusk, and into the night. And when we ran out of voice (not words or ideas—we never ran out of those) I prowled among his files, or read his current correspondence, or his work in progress, to all of which he gave me unrestricted access.

Rex further provided me with a letter of introduction to his kin, friends, and associates. "Include warts," he told them, and the number of letters I wrote grew and grew till the total went past the four thousand mark. Many of those I wrote to I met subsequently and interviewed in depth. And always, his wife, Pola, his two daughters, Barbara and Rebecca, and his sisters Ruth and Mary (like himself nearing ninety), gladly received me, counseled me, and shared with me precious letters, documents, photographs, and insights nurtured in their love and understanding of Rex Stout.

A few weeks before his death Rex told me that he was under a psychological compulsion not to be older than fifty-eight when he was with anybody. He was then on the eve of his eighty-ninth birthday, but he was not deceiving himself. To the end his mind was that of a man in his prime. Indeed, in the last year of his life, he wrote, in eight weeks, *A Family Affair*, the novel with which he closed his ten thousand page saga of Nero Wolfe, told in seventy-two tales, the first of them written forty-two years earlier when he was already forty-seven.

Rex Doesn't sound fifty-eight in *A Family Affair*. Indeed, he sounds thirty-four, for that was the age he assigned permanently to Archie Goodwin, who narrates the Nero Wolfe stories. No one reading *A Family Affair* would suspect that it had been written by a man nearing ninety. "Rex," Clifton Fadiman told me, "has an IQ of a hundred and eighty-five." Perhaps that was to be expected of a man who was a collateral descendant both of Daniel Defoe and Benjamin Franklin. Even so, it seems incredible that he held together as he did, and that, at eighty-nine, as had been true all his life, he could produce a book the first draft of which was also the final draft. This is literally so. Rex Stout never put a word on paper until he knew what he wanted to say. No revision was ever necessary. His publishers set up in print, as received, the one and only draft of his books.

At the time of his death, 27 October 1975, Rex had fifty-seven books in print, more than any other living American writer. These books had sold in excess of a hundred million copies and had been translated into twenty-six languages. CBS hailed him as "the American Conan Doyle." The London *Times* said that of the authors writing in English, Agatha Christie alone outsold him behind the Iron Curtain. In the *New York Times* his death was front-page news. He had, the world press agreed, created one of the immortals of detective fiction. "His," said Ian Fleming, "was one of the most civilized minds to turn to detective fiction." The scope of his readership supported this assertion. Even Rex himself found it astonishing. He had letters from bankers, college presidents, nonagenarians, teenagers, men and women in prison, telegraphers, Hollywood movie stars, editors, actuaries, micro-biologists, nuclear physicists, GIs, waitresses, dog trainers, and the father of cybernetics, M.I.T.'s Nobert Wiener. He still had other fan letters from Justice Oliver Wendell Holmes, Franklin Roosevelt, Dwight Eisenhower, Bertrand Russell, Havelock Ellis, Aldous Huxley, Graham Greene, Georges Simenon, Cardinal Wright, Hubert Humphrey, Giscard d'Estaing, Robert Penn Warren, John Wayne, Tip O'Neill, P.G. Wodehouse, Agatha Christie, J.B. Priestly, Leon Edel, William Faulkner, John Steinbeck, Oscar Hammerstein II, Henry Miller, Ross Macdonald, Ellery Queen, Robert Parker, Alfred Lunt and Lynn Fontane, Norman Cousins, Marlene Dietrich, and the Maharajah of Indore.

Order was essential in Rex's peace of mind. By temperament he was a scheduler. Every Sunday, without fail, I sent him a questionnaire, supplementing the questions I put to him during our frequent summit meetings at High Meadow. He caught my rhythms and incorporated me into his schedule. Over one hundred and eighty-seven weeks he dutifully answered and returned to me one hundred and eighty-seven questionnaires, answering, in all, more than seventy-five hundred questions. I did learn to give him a week off while the World Series was on, and to announce my visits three days in advance. "I'm still breathing," he would say, "come ahead."

Letters came from him, too, at a steady rate—in all, more than four hundred of them.

At the outset I sometimes misjudged Rex's mindset. I conjectured for example, that money meant nothing to him. After all, he had given away hundreds of thousands of dollars to the causes he held dear—the war against Hitler, the Writers War Board (which he headed up for four years, while taking no salary), Freedom House, the Writers Board for World Government, the United World Federalists, the Society for the Prevention of World War III, Amnesty International, the Authors League, and the Authors Guild. "You couldn't be more wrong," he said. "Money provides all of my freedom and many of my pleasures." Another time I surmised that his pithy letters were the product of concentrated effort. "I'll give them a few seconds," he said. Eventually I could predict the substance of his answers before he made them. For example, Rex on seat belts: "Wearing a seat belt is like wearing a helmet through town on the chance that someone might drop something on your head." On motorcycles: "I sneer at them."

I think Rex kept a fever chart on me for several months after I officially got to work on the authorized biography. He chided me once for spelling "okay" with an "e." He was shocked when I owned up that I didn't know how many nipples were on a cow's udder. How could a man with a Ph.D. from Harvard not know a basic fact like that? If I phrased a question badly he answered it but put the offending phrase in quotation marks to remind me that it was not *his*.

Rex hated pretense. If you didn't understand something, for example the working of the school banking system that he invented and realized half a million dollars on before he was forty, or the complex reorganization of the Authors League, which he undertook and carried out when he was seventy-seven, it was best to say so. He would explain it patiently and stay with it until you had it clear in your mind. "He never makes you feel like a dumbbell," his daughter Rebecca told me. That was quite true.

Though not easy to impress, Rex respected thoroughness. He guffawed when I came up with the real identity of Lieutenant Rowcliff—a well-guarded secret. And when I located, in an auto motor court, in Springfield, Massachusetts, the venerable Julia Sanderson (his girl friend in the Teddy Roosevelt era), thunderstruck for once, he said, "You have *found* Julia Sanderson!" After that he used to say to me, "You're one hell of a research man."

I was not a surrogate son but we were companionable and I was his confidant. And when I'd be leaving, after a visit, he would stand in the drive to watch me out of his sight and, at my last handwave, throw a kiss from his fingertips, with the grave dignity of a venerable hidalgo seeing off a favorite nephew to New Spain. That is what Rex was like.

Archie was Rex's spontaneous self. Wolfe was his achieved self. Sometimes I could be Archie to his Wolfe. I could never be Wolfe to his Archie. I could banter with him, but I could not counsel him. I doubt if anyone ever could. If Rex's authority was Neronian, his sense of fun was Goodwinian. Awareness of this fact was basic to understanding of how his mind worked. "Nothing is too big, too grand, or too sacred to have its funny aspects," he told me. Take the day his secretary came to work in a snit. Rex retired into his office and, after a few minutes, rang for her, handing her, when she appeared, a large pink disc which he had just cut from cardboard. On it he had written "Reward for Sharp Retort." The girl laughed and her testiness was forgotten, but not his gesture. Fifty years later she remembered it with delight. During his final summer Rex did not visit his beloved garden too often. One day, when he did go there, he wrote to Rebecca, in California. "The day lilies said to me 'You again? We thought you were gone for good.' I told them I wasn't even gone for bad."

In *Please Pass the Guilt* a client asks Wolfe, "How many things have *you* done that you wouldn't want everyone to know about?" Wolfe answers, "Perhaps a thousand." When I read that I said to Rex, "I know a thousand things you've done that you wouldn't want everyone to know about. What shall I do with them?" "Put them in," he said, "they'll probably be the most interesting things in the book." Before he died he read the whole manuscript. He took out nothing to spare his vanity. He did not survive to see the book win the Edgar Allan Poe Award for biography in 1978, but the award was his as much as mine. With Rex being the person he was how could I lose?

When I finished *Rex Stout: A Biography* I had five filing cabinets filled with notes—twenty-five yards of files. Inevitably much of the material I had collected never got into the book. But much of it is too good to be buried. There's a Wolfe Pack, an international Rex Stout organization with hundreds of members. For many years, as a contributing editor, I wrote the *Rex Stout Newsletter* for *The Armchair Detective*. There's a *Nero Wolfe Handbook* and a *Nero Wolfe Gazette*, which features, among other things, Wolfe, Archie, and Rex web site updates. Recently, A&E launched a successful Wolfe series. In the fall of 2001 I received a letter from James A. Rock & Company Publishers inquiring about the biography and the inquiries have led to a fifth edition, published under its new title *Rex Stout: A Majesty's Life*.

Along with P.G. Wodehouse's original Foreword, this new edition contains my new Millennial Introduction and an Afterword by my son Andrew who visited High Meadow as a boy.

Rex once told me that his works would long be forgotten by the new millennium. He never specified which new millennium however. Read on.

Boston College, 2003
Chestnut Hill, Massachusetts

Conversations
with Rex Stout

Nero Wolfe's fight against crime spans some five decades (seven if you count Robert Goldsborough's excellent continuation of the series) with the rotund detective first appearing on the scene in 1933 (*Fer-de-Lance*) testing prohibition beer and when last beheld, in 1975, he was deploring the outrage of Watergate (*A Family Affair*). Rex Stout died on October 27, 1975. More than three decades after his death fans of crime literature all over the world still take delight in his craft.

The following are some of my father's most memorable and informative conversations with Rex Stout and shortly before my father's death, he and I selected them especially for connoisseurs of crime fiction (from *Royal Decree,* Pontes Press, 1983).

—Andrew McAleer

McAleer: When you were writing for the pulps, between nineteen twelve and nineteen seventeen, did you see yourself as a hack writer or as an aspiring young writer on his way to the top?

Stout: I have never regarded myself as this or that. I have been too busy being myself to bother about regarding myself.

McAleer: Julian Symons says the Holmes series falls off in the last two collections?

Stout: Symons? I don't know him. I don't agree with him either. I think one or two of the later Holmes stories are among the best.

McAleer: Anthony Burgess says that those who write series detective stories are artists—like Wodehouse and Faulkner—building a world. Do you agree?

Stout: Depends on the writer. Conan Doyle and Simenon yes; Christie or Gardner, no.

McAleer: I take it that Conan Doyle is one of your passions?

Stout: Every Sherlock Holmes story has at least one marvelous scene. And there's Holmes himself. Doyle stokes in a thousand shrewd touches with no effort at all. Wonderful.

McAleer: Did Archie hang up the picture of Sherlock Holmes that is found over his desk, or did Wolfe put it there?

Stout: Did I say that at one point? I was a damn fool to do it. Obviously it is always an artistic fault in any fiction to mention any other character in fiction. It should never be done.

McAleer: Your culprits always capitulate plausibly. Do you take care to see that they do?

Stout: Everything in a story should be credible, but one of the hardest things to believe is that anyone will abandon the effort to escape a charge of murder. Therefore it is extremely important to "suspend disbelief" on that. If you don't, the story is spoiled.

McAleer: Simenon says characters must never be too thought out or willed. Is he right?

Stout: A character who is thought out is not born, he or she is contrived. A born character is round, a thought out character is flat.

McAleer: How do you control your novelettes so that they seem just as intricate and entire as your novels?

Stout: You might as well ask a shortstop how he avoids tripping when he whirls to throw.

McAleer: Is a novelette easier to write than a novel?

Stout: In a way, short fiction is harder to write than long. An unnecessary page in a long novel doesn't hurt it much, but an unnecessary sentence in a three-thousand-word story spoils it.

McAleer: Steven Marcus, a professor at Columbia, says that Dashiell Hammett, by a succession of "complex devices. . .was able to raise the crime story into literature." Is he right?

Stout: "Raise?" No. It had been done before, for instance by Collins and Poe.

McAleer: Yet you hold Hammett in high regard?

Stout: Certainly. He was better than Chandler, though to read the critics you wouldn't think so. In fact, *The Glass Key* is better than anything Hemingway ever wrote … Hemingway never grew out of adolescence. His scope and depth stayed shallow because he had no idea what women are for. I think he was a latent homosexual and hated himself for it.

McAleer: Kingsley Amis says that you must be as Johnsonian as Wolfe is, that is, "a moralist before anything else." Do you accept this estimate?

Stout: I am not any kind of an "ist." I have a strong moral sense—by *my* standards.

McAleer: Kingsley Amis thinks that Wolfe's speech carries the flavor of the eighteenth century. Do you think so, too?

Stout: No.

McAleer: How many times have you read Boswell's life of Samuel Johnson?

Stout: All of it, twice.

McAleer: Amis sees Wolfe as a latter-day Samuel Johnson. Do you find that an agreeable compliment?

Stout: Yes. Since I like Johnson, I'd like to think that Wolfe invites comparison with him.

McAleer: To many readers Wolfe is the epitome of the rational man.

Stout: If they want to feel that way, God bless 'em. They'll probably buy another book, and that's all I care about.

McAleer: Then you don't think man is a rational animal?

Stout: The minute those two little particles inside a woman's womb have joined together billions of decisions have been made. A thing like that has to come from entropy. All men are reasoning animals more than any other animal. Of course they are. That's perfectly obvious. They have a bigger brain and a better brain. And we reason with our brain. But to say that man is reasoning animal is a very different thing than to say that most of man's decisions are based on his rational process. That I don't believe at all. But of course he's a rational animal. He damn well better be in this complicated world, believe me, or he isn't going to last very long.

McAleer: Do Wolfe and Archie represent the struggle between reason and instinct?

Stout: No. Readers seldom give a damn what characters illustrate, or whether they illustrate anything. The reason they are more interested in my characters than in my plots is that the characters seem real to them and engage their emotions and concerns just as "real" people do. Most characters in stories don't do that. I haven't any idea why and how I have created characters who do.

McAleer: *P.S. Magazine* says that Wolfe is "lovable." Do you accept that term?

Stout: No.

McAleer: What is your opinion of Bernard Shaw?

Stout: One of the cleverest men that ever lived and I just can't stand him. I had lunch with him once. He was such a goddamn smartaleck.

McAleer: Did you ever read Carroll John Daly's *The Third Murderer*? It features a New York police inspector who chews an unlighted cigar like your Inspector Cramer. Unlike Cramer, however, he turns out to be the murderer.

Stout: I've never read anything by Daly. He wrote for *Black Mask*. I never read *Black Mask* either.

McAleer: Do you ever outline a story before starting to write?

Stout: I never block stories—sometimes the idea comes from a situation that interests me. Once I wanted to get Wolfe connected with a baby. *The Mother Hunt* came from that.

> —John McAleer
> *High Meadow, Connecticut/New York*
> *1972-1975 home of Rex Stout*
> Boston College, Revisited 2003

A Short Essay on Writers Influencing Writers

Andrew McAleer

This article first appeared in *Reflections in A Private Eye,*
Vol. 22, No. 4, December 2002 as "Ross Macdonald's
Belgium-French Connection."

The question of whether or not Dashiell Hammett
and Raymond Chandler influenced Ross Macdonald can
be answered simply: They did. But how Macdonald
managed to break from the masters may not be as easily
answered.

Larry N. Landrum's biography of Macdonald in the
indispensable *Twentieth Century Crime and Mystery Writers* (St. Martin's press, 1980) reminds devotees: "The
texture of the world in this novel [*Blue City*] is reminiscent
of Dashiell Hammett's fiction, though its sensibility and
imagery show the influence of Raymond Chandler."

Macdonald, primarily through the voice of his Santa
Teresa private investigator, Lew Archer, would eventually distinguish himself from Hammett and Chandler.
Discussed below is one likely influence that may have
contributed to the author's literary achievement.

In *20th* Landrum also addresses Macdonald's break
from Chandler by noting that Macdonald defined, *The
Doomsters* (1958) as, "a fairly clean break with the Chandler tradition." What follows hereafter for Macdonald
is the "psychological view of crime," "conflicts of social
change," and, among other things, "familial dissension."

Lew Archer becomes, in Landrum's nomenclature, "…
a window into ourselves." Further, Macdonald, "move[d]
his fiction back toward the class assumptions of British
detective fiction that Hammett and Chandler had re-
jected." Notwithstanding, the British may not have sin-
gular claim to Macdonald achieving: "a greater truth
and higher art," in crime literature.

Belgian-French detective fiction, through the works
of Georges Simenon, (Belgian born, yet French is the
chief language for much of Belgium) quite possibly made
some contribution to Macdonald's successful transition.

In *The Blue Hammer* (1976), Macdonald describes
rush hour this way: "There was fairly heavy traffic at
this mid-evening hour, crawling like an endless lumi-
nescent worm into the tunneled darkness." P. 175 Knopf.

Now, let's abandon the automobile and allow
Simenon to roll things back to the golden age of train
travel and detective fiction.

In *The Crossroads Murders* (1933), Inspector
Maigret's creator characterizes night travel in this manner: "Soon the night swallowed up the little red light at
the rear of the big vehicle. In the distance a train moved
across the landscape like an improbable, luminous cat-
erpillar." P. 67 Covici, Friede.

It is possible that Macdonald merely re-worked one of
his peer's similes and then moved on, but such a solution
does not seem possible when the similarities between the
Paris and Santa Teresa narratives are considered.

When assessing the Maigret stories Edward L.
Galligan in *The South Atlantic Quarterly*, makes the following observations: "The Maigret stories reveal the fundamental qualities of Simenon's mind; nearly all of them

are, in a sense, fables demonstrating the ways of the creative, or intuitive, intelligence ... Much more concerned with the why's of murder than with the who's, the Maigrets are perceptive about the realities of human behavior."

And when Robert F. Moss in *The Scribner Mystery & Suspense Writers* (1998) considers Archer he tells us, "He is ... a searcher who probes the complex relationships among people and attempts to discover the truth of what has happened and, more important, why it happened." In addition, Moss asserts, "He [Macdonald] adopted the form as created by Chandler and Hammett and modified it to reflect his own experiences, sensibility, and perceptions of human behavior."

In the *Oxford Companion to Crime and Mystery Writing* J. Randolph Cox takes this position regarding Maigret: "Maigret does not solve crimes by making logical deductions based on shrewd observation, but rather by his patience and ability to understand human nature." In the same Oxford volume Jesse Berret holds, "Archer becomes less interested in meting out justice than in simply listening to and understanding others."

In various forms, psychology entered the lives of Simenon and Macdonald and such a connection may offer a fair explanation concerning the overwhelming, sometimes verbatim critical analysis of their works. But even if this per chance psychological nexus did play some role in Macdonald's leap, the Simenon connection at least raises the question as to whether or not it was separate and distinct.

For dedicated crime fiction connoisseurs, the idea of a Simenon contribution to Macdonald ought to warrant serious thought. But don't consider the idea alone. Fetch a long British draft and ponder this notion along with Archer and Maigret. Select any volume. You can't miss.

ABOUT THE AUTHORS

John McAleer is the Edgar Allan Poe Award-winning author of *Rex Stout: A Biography* and a best-selling author of fifteen other books including the critically-acclaimed mystery, *Coign of Vantage*. A Professor of English Literature at Harvard and, later, Boston College for more than half a century, Professor McAleer also worked as an editor of *The Armchair Detective,* served as a vice president of the Mystery Writers of America and was nominated for the Pulitzer Prize.

Andrew McAleer is the author of three mystery novels and serves as the president of America's oldest continuing literary society, the Boston Authors Club. He teaches Crime Fiction at Boston College, is a member of the Private Eye Writers of America, the editor of the award-winning *Crimestalker Casebook* and a recipient of the Sherlock Holmes Revere Bowl Award. Mr. McAleer practices law privately in Massachusetts.

Edward D. Hoch is a Mystery Writers of America Grand Master, an Edgar Allan Poe Award-winning author and one of the most prolific writers in the crime fiction genre. A tireless contributor to *Ellery Queen Mystery Magazine,* Mr. Hoch served as president of the MWA and was the 1991 guest of honor at Bouchercon.

CPSIA information can be obtained at www.ICGtesting.com
Printed in the USA
BVOW020139310812

299204BV00013B/1/A

9 781596 635050